Pat [illegible] and
to helping you with all
your real estate needs.
Diane

Home Selling Sharks

Eat Your Home's Equity

Diane Cardano-Casacio

Home Selling Sharks

Created with:
90-Minute Books
302 Martinique Drive
Winter Haven, FL 33884
www.90minutebooks.com

Copyright © 2018, Diane Cardano-Casacio

Published in the United States of America

161109-00608-2
ISBN: 9781795009355
Imprint: Independently published

For more information on 90-Minute Books including finding out how you
can publish your own book, visit 90minutebooks.com or call (863) 318-0464

Here's What's Inside...

Introduction

Would you jump into a pool of man-eating sharks without the protection of a cage? When it comes to real estate, thousands of home sellers do just that. They jump into selling their home without protecting themselves from the Home Selling Sharks. That's what this book is about.

You might be wondering, what are Home Selling Sharks? What do they do? Home Selling Sharks are things that negatively impact the sale of your home. They're lurking all around your home right now, waiting to eat away at your equity and, worse, cause your home not to sell!

Why do people try to swim with these Home Selling Sharks without any protection? Well, they think they know everything or they just don't know any better. They've heard an advertisement on the radio; read articles on Realtor.com, Zillow, or other real estate websites; watched HGTV; or they simply don't trust Realtors®. They think they can swim faster than the sharks, but the water is too dark and they can't see the sharks coming for them. Thousands of home sellers do this every day.

I've written this book to protect you from these Home Selling Sharks. It's a good thing you've taken the initiative to start reading my proven strategies for home selling success to avoid being bitten by the Home Selling Sharks and losing a lot of money. I call these my 8 Secret Strategies and by following them, I guarantee you'll keep up to 10% more money in your pocket, sell your home four times faster than average, and enjoy a stress-free sale. If you're a home seller who wants to sell your home for the most money, in the shortest length of time, and with the least amount of hassle, it's vital you avoid the Home Selling Sharks and follow the steps I've outlined in this book.

Leo was one such seller. He had done his research by attending one of my home seller seminars. Over the years after the seminar, I had stayed in touch with Leo and kept him advised of the current trends in the real estate market. Then one brisk October day, Leo called me. While it's not uncommon for my past seminar graduates to call with questions, this time it was different. Leo knew it was time to sell. He had journeyed the path to become at peace with closing the chapter of his life called "his home," and he wanted his investment to pay off.

Leo was the perfect student. He was able to step back and remove himself from the emotional connection to his property and treat his home as an asset. Most importantly, Leo was coachable and allowed me to implement my 8 Secret Strategies. He followed every piece of advice, down to showing his home with an immaculate, empty, and freshly painted garage and basement. Imagine that!

Leo was the typical empty nester with 90% to 100% equity in his home, and it was one of the largest assets in his financial portfolio. He needed every penny from the sale of his home to move into a retirement community and enough money left over to travel and enjoy his wonder years. Ultimately, he wanted to sell his home quickly, stress-free, and for top dollar. Does this sound like you?

Throughout this book, I'll be explaining the 8 Secret Strategies that are essential when listing a home for sale and keeping the Home Selling Sharks out of your home. I'll also detail how Leo used these strategies to sell his house in two days for $21,000 more than his asking price. My commitment is that every one of my home seller clients and every avid reader of my book will have the same goals Leo did: start the home selling process earlier than you think you need to, differentiate your home to crush the competition, and have buyers lined up outside the door.

I am passionate about helping home owners like Leo sell their homes fast, hassle-free, and for the most money. Why? Simply put, there's another way of selling that's different from what traditional real estate companies offer. My goal is that after you've read this book, you will pass it down to future home sellers you know so they can explore all their options before selling their home. I also want all home sellers to understand how important researching their options is to their bottom line. With some research and the right marketing strategy, you can steer clear of home selling obstacles without a bite from any of the Home Selling Sharks and, most importantly, with money left in your pocket.

To your success!

Diane

Chapter 1
Why Do Some Homes Not Sell for Top Dollar or Seem to Take Forever to Sell?

There are a myriad of Home Selling Sharks that can cost sellers thousands of dollars and cause them to lose valuable marketing time. Do you want to be bitten by one and lose thousands? If not, keep reading! Most home sellers don't know what they don't know when it comes to avoiding these shark-biting home selling obstacles. Problems can arise months and years before going on the market. These problems end up causing more issues during the sales process that can negatively impact your bottom line. Therefore, it's important for anyone selling a home to be aware and informed of the hazards to avoid. Let's take a look at the top 8 Home Selling Sharks lying in wait, seeking to attack unsuspecting sellers like you and take huge bites out of your equity.

Shark #1: Realty Shark

One common mistake occurs when home sellers hire a friend, family member, or someone unqualified for the job of marketing and selling their home. Think about it, would you hire your friend who just became a doctor to perform heart surgery on you? I don't think so. Unfortunately, many home sellers don't know what to look for when hiring a Realtor®. They often hire the wrong person to sell one of their largest assets. Even worse, they're stuck in a six-month or one-year contract.

When you're interviewing real estate agents, it's important to understand what you need to look for and the questions to ask, so you can hire an expert Realtor® and evade a bite from the Realty Shark. Throughout this book, I'll be referring to Realtors® because these are the only real estate consultants you should ever consider hiring. Beware of hiring a real estate licensee who is not a member of the National Association of Realtors (NAR). He or she will not have the official Realtor® designation and won't be committed to following NAR's guidelines and ethics. How committed can they be if they don't want to spend a few hundred dollars to be part of the industry's premier organization? The Realty Shark has the biggest bite and can cause you to lose thousands. Don't let this happen to you! **(Learn how to avoid the Realty Shark in Chapter 3.)**

Shark #2: Inspection Shark

Most sellers don't have their home inspected *before* they put their property on the market, so they don't know what troubles are hiding inside and outside of their home. Instead, the inspection is completed only after the buyer and seller agree on a price. Problems with the home are revealed and it's too late. Buyers request an exorbitant number of repairs, demand to lower the price, or both! Boom, there go thousands of dollars! What's more, at this point in the process, the buyer will often back out of the deal. This shark can really draw some blood and take big bites out of your equity. **(Learn how to avoid the Inspection Shark in Chapter 4.)**

Shark #3: Photography Shark

When buyers are searching online for a home, photos are the first impression. Since 99.9% of buyers use the Internet to find a home, exterior and interior pictures will determine whether a buyer requests more information on your home instead of your competitor's home. If you don't have the best quality photos taken from the most marketable angles, prospective buyers will just move on to the next property listing. Buyers bypass the home because the photos don't grab their attention. Additionally, bad photography leads to your property being displayed poorly in front of millions of viewers.

This shark is deadly and causes your home to stay on the market much longer than it should, ultimately costing you thousands of dollars. **(Learn how to avoid the Photography Shark in Chapter 5.)**

Shark #4: Staging Shark

Another reason why some homes don't sell quickly or for top dollar is that sellers don't have a plan of action and they don't prepare early enough. They've painted their rooms the wrong color, they've spent money on upgrades that won't bring value, and they have so much stuff accumulated over the years they don't know where to start. When buyers don't like how a home looks online, they move on to the next home. It's like shopping for clothes or shoes. What happens to spring clothes that don't sell during the spring season? They end up on the fall clearance rack, right? You do not want this happening to your home! You don't want your home to be on the market for months just to be listed at a discounted price later on. Then you'll be forced to take any offer that comes your way. This shark hurts badly, but it's the simplest one to overcome. **(Learn how to avoid the Staging Shark in Chapter 6.)**

Shark #5: Marketing Shark

Poor marketing causes listings to stay on the market indefinitely, leading to stagnation and lack of buyer interest. Homes that are not advertised on enough websites and have no customized marketing plan in place, wind up in the jaws of the Marketing Shark. Additionally, most Realtors® don't spend any money advertising homes and neither does their company. Therefore, you're left with only a few buyers viewing your property. This shark also attracts lowball offers from buyers. Why? Poor marketing doesn't allow buyers to see your home's value, hence less money in your pocket. **(Learn how to avoid the Marketing Shark in Chapter 7.)**

Shark #6: Pre-Marketing Shark

Establishing an initial momentum is essential for expertly marketing a home. However, most Realtors® don't showcase a seller's home online *before* the listing goes on the market. They simply put a sign on the lawn, a lockbox on the door, and wait for someone else to sell it. There is no "Coming Soon" buzz created, like movie trailers entice the public to get excited about a new film. This lack of excitement prior to the property being listed for sale in the Multiple Listing Service equates to fewer buyers lined up in front of the property once the house hits the market and, inevitably, your home stays on the market for months versus days. **(Learn how to avoid the Pre-Marketing Shark in Chapter 8.)**

Shark #7: Pricing Shark

Pricing is another common issue that causes countless homes to stay on the market. Many real estate agents don't accurately price a seller's property. They overvalue the home to get the listing. And because the home is overpriced, it stays on the market too long. Then the Realtor's® only strategy is to place a price reduced sign on the lawn, a dreadful sign of desperation. Find out how to fight this shark by understanding which factors affect the value of your home. Plus, learn how to recognize inaccurate comparable sales and avoid relying on them to determine your home's listing price. **(Learn how to avoid the Pricing Shark in Chapter 9.)**

Shark #8: Showtime Shark

Unfortunately, many Realtors® rush to get a property on the market instead of strategizing the on-the-market date to build demand. They don't know about the Showtime Shark. They add a new listing into the Multiple Listing Service (MLS) without a formulated plan in place and no designated day for initial showings. Potential buyers start touring the home any day of the week, while other buyers, who may have been willing to pay you more, never get a chance to see your property. The first showing sets the tone for what's to come. Without that initial momentum and interest from multiple buyers, sellers are left to flounder, accepting an offer without weighing all their options and losing thousands. **(Learn how to avoid the Showtime Shark in Chapter 10.)**

In the next chapters, I'll detail my 8 Secret Strategies, which address how you can overcome these Home Selling Sharks and the many others obstacles that cause properties not to sell. That is, if you want to sell your home quickly, stress-free, and for top dollar. That's the idea, isn't it? So I leave the ball in your court. Read this book, only if you want more dollars in your pocket when you leave the settlement table.

Chapter 2
How to Fight the Home Selling Sharks

When you're selling your home, it's important to
know that there's an option that doesn't include
the traditional Realtor's® practices. In this new
world of real estate, "traditional" methods do not
give you the opportunity to maximize your
financial return on your investment. For the
majority of home sellers, their home is the
largest asset in their financial portfolio.
Therefore, to keep money in your pocket, it's
critical to fight the Home Selling Sharks.
Unfortunately, just one mistake could cost you a
lot of money. One shark bite here, another bite
there, and before you know it, you've lost
thousands of dollars. You can, however, avoid
these bites and fight the Home Selling Sharks
lurking in your home, waiting to eat away at your
equity.

All you need to do is implement the 8 Secret Strategies outlined in this book and have the following essential mindset:

1. Start earlier than you think you need to, so you can
2. Crush your competition and
3. Have buyers lined up outside your door.

You cannot implement the 8 Secret Strategies without this foundation. Let's break down the components of this concept:

1. Start Earlier Than You Think You Need To

People are very busy today and often times don't plan their home selling process. They wake up, call a Realtor® who's a friend, family member, an acquaintance, or a neighbor, and then go on the market. They wait until the last minute to start the home selling process. The problem with that is there's no specific, organized plan for selling.

What's more, you can't go back in time to do the things you could have done if you had started earlier to plan the home selling process. You'll lose thousands of dollars because you never had the opportunity to implement the 8 Secret Strategies, especially the first four, which are critical to the process of selling your home.

The ideal time to start the process of preparing your home for sale is at least two years in advance of when you're actually ready to go on the market and, at the very least, 6 months to one year in advance.

Think about it. What if a sudden issue arises that forces you to sell immediately, such as a health or financial problem? You simply will not be ready and you're guaranteed to lose thousands because you are not prepared. Are you beginning to understand how starting early can help you be more prepared to market your property and fight the Home Selling Sharks? Your home is one of your largest assets after all, isn't it? So be sure to plan ahead so you can keep as much equity as possible from your home sale.

How do I know that starting early can keep money in your pocket? Since 2008, I have been holding quarterly home seller seminars. My seminar graduates have had extraordinary success with their home selling process. As a matter of fact, on average, my seminar graduates' homes stay on the market for only 13 days, well within my 26-day home sold guarantee. Also, selling faster also means more money in their pocket, with many selling their homes over the listed price!

Why do my seminar grads have this added success? Because they started much earlier than they thought they needed to by coming to a seminar.

They came to a seminar at least six months to three years in advance. They learned about the entire home selling process from start to finish and met other people who had success with these 8 Secret Strategies.

I've developed an exclusive website for readers of my book, **www.HomeSellingSharksBook.com**. Here, you can sign up for one of my seminars, where I teach future home sellers my 8 Secret Strategies, as well as access a wealth of information about the home selling process.

2. Crush the Competition

When selling your home, it's important to have the mindset to crush your competition, unless you want your home to sit on the market 120 days, 180 days, one year, or worse, never sell at all. Sellers who follow the 8 Secret Strategies to fight the Home Selling Sharks will learn what it takes to set their home apart from the competition and sell within 26 days. If you want to stay on the market for months and months, stop reading right now. This book is definitely not for you.

To gain an edge over the competition when you sell your home, you must start earlier than you think you need to, so you can build up demand for your property. This will lead to a larger return on your investment. Isn't that what it's all about?

Imagine a basketball game where the home team scored 101 points for a landslide victory over the visiting team, who only scored three points. Wouldn't you say the home team crushed the competition? This score would definitely grab a sports writer's attention and lead to an impressive newspaper article. You too can be on the winning side of the home selling process by having this vision of crushing the competition when selling your home.

3. Have Buyers Lined Up Outside the Door

Imagine people lined up outside your door with their checkbooks the very first day your home opens for showings. You don't think this can happen? I've sold thousands of homes since 1993. Using my 8 Secret Strategies, 95% of my listings sell within 26 days and 55% sell the first weekend on the market, with buyers lined up outside the door. By following the strategies outlined in this book, you'll have buyers begging to get into your home, just waiting to pay you list price and even more. Now that is a vision!

Now that you understand the sharks lurking around your property as well as the mindset you need to market your home, it's time to cover the 8 Secret Strategies necessary to fight the sharks. I'll show you how my home selling client Leo followed each of these strategies to sell his home quickly and for thousands over his initial Coming Soon listing price.

Only continue reading if you're serious about keeping money in your pocket. Please be open-minded about the possibilities and about learning what you don't know that you don't know.

Chapter 3
Strategy #1 for Fighting the Home Selling Sharks: Marketing & Negotiating Expertise

The first strategy to fight the Home Selling Sharks is to hire a real estate company with an expert marketer and negotiator who also has a broker's license. The company you hire should also have licensed specialists working behind the scenes overseeing all the details of a listing.

This is exactly what my client Leo wanted, a real estate marketing expert experienced in negotiating aggressively day in and day out, so he could get every penny he deserved from the sale of his home. As a result, he hired me and my team to implement our proven systems that would give him the opportunity to keep his equity and guarantee

the sale of his home within 26 days. Having
attended my seminar, he knew he should start
early, so he called us one year in advance of selling
his home.

Now this is different than a traditional real estate
company, right? Those companies are filled with
hundreds of agents who are not marketing
experts. Statistics show an average agent only
sells four houses per year. How good of a
negotiator can they be in protecting your
number one asset? A few weekends of training
and about $600 is all it takes to get a real estate
license. However, home sellers need and deserve
more than a traditional Realtor® who simply has
a real estate salesperson license and lacks a
marketing degree, a negotiating credential, and a
broker's license.

To top it off, most of these traditional agents
work for franchise real estate companies that are
being bought out by corporations and business
tycoons. As a result, these companies spend
thousands of dollars on TV and radio ads,
marketing themselves, not their sellers'
properties. They want to get as many home
sellers as possible to sign a listing contract in
hopes that some of the homes sell, so they get
paid. However, the traditional company pays
about 70% to 90% commission to the agent. Paid
by whom? By you, the seller! Therefore, after
paying support staff and other office expenses,
these companies have no money left to spend
marketing your home.

There are hundreds of these types of companies, and I'm sure you've heard of them: RE/MAX, Coldwell Banker, Berkshire Hathaway-Fox & Roach, Keller Williams, Weichert, etc. So how can these real estate corporations make money? By getting as many Realtors® in the office to sell, sell, sell, that's how! Plus, they make money by charging Realtors® a monthly management fee, an administrative fee, a copy fee, an Internet fee and more. Because they own the title and mortgage companies, they also capitalize on titles, mortgages, and other components.

Consequently, for every transaction, they're making an additional $5,000-$10,000 or more. It's a profitable gambit and one that completely ignores the consumer's experience. For these companies, it is nothing more than a numbers game.

Let's look at an example: Warren Buffett bought out many real estate offices, now called Berkshire Hathaway. Do you think Warren Buffett is sitting around worrying about how much money he should spend marketing your home? Does Warren Buffett care if your home gets sold or not? I don't think so.

5 Most Common Mistakes Sellers Make When Choosing a Realtor®

As I mentioned in the first chapter, there are major mistakes or issues, I call them Home Selling Sharks, that cause home sellers to lose thousands of dollars. However, all of these sharks can be avoided by hiring the right real estate consultant, a Realtor® who is an expert in marketing and negotiating. So how can you find the most qualified person for the very important job of selling your most prized asset?

Let's look at the most common errors home sellers make when choosing a Realtor® to market and sell their home. Then I'll provide you with information on how to recognize an expert Realtor® from these traditional Realtors®.

Mistake #1 – Hiring a Family Member or Friend

Many of the home sellers I work with had their home on the market for six months or more with another Realtor®, and the home did not sell. They hired a Realtor® who was a family member, a friend, or someone from an organization they were affiliated with because they felt obligated. Would you hand over your number one asset to someone without marketing or negotiating experience just because they're a friend or family member? You'd be surprised. Many home sellers do just that.

To avoid this mistake, do your homework and know what the profile of an expert Realtor® looks like. Interview a few Realtors® on the phone prior to bringing them into your home. Interview them using the same questions so you can measure them equally.

Once you've completed your interviews, invite two Realtors® into your home who best match the profile of a marketing and negotiating expert so they can show you exactly how they're going to market your property for sale. Don't go with the Realtor® you like the most. Hire the Realtor® who isn't afraid to tell you exactly what needs to be done. You do not want any fake news at this most critical part of the process!

Go to **www.HomeSellingSharksBook.com** and see Strategy #1: Marketing and Negotiating Expertise to find a list of questions to ask a Realtor® before hiring one. For each question, I'll provide you with the appropriate answer that a Realtor® should give based on the profile of an expert. Visit the website and see Strategy #1: Marketing and Negotiating Expertise for the most up-to-date information.

If you don't have Internet access and would like my team to send you my list of questions to ask a Realtor® and the answers an expert should give, complete the mail-in form located in the appendix or call **215-576-8666**.

Mistake #2- Hiring a Real Estate Company with Lots of Signs on Lawns

Traditional real estate companies hire anyone with a license in hopes they'll sell one or two homes. These companies have lots of signs on lawns because they want to attract agents to work for them. They're not interested in marketing your property. They're interested in building their work pool. And these companies have hundreds of agents working in their offices.

Unfortunately, many home sellers hire a Realtor® because the Realtor® is affiliated with a company that has lots of lawn signs. What many home sellers don't know is that signs don't bring buyers because most buyers are searching for homes online, on Zillow, Trulia, and Realtor.com. They don't call on signs anymore.

If they do see a lawn sign, they look up the property online to view pictures of the home's interior to decide whether or not they want to view the property. If they happen to call for more information about your home, the call goes to the agent on floor time. Agents on floor time sit in the office for a two-hour period, waiting for buyers to call or email for more information about a home. Generally, these agents are newer agents who need business and are also the least experienced in real estate.

So now you've hired a real estate company with lots of signs on the lawns, the agent has no marketing or negotiating expertise, and calls or emails from very interested buyers are being handled by the least experienced salespeople in the company. Don't let this happen to you!

Do you really want to hire a company with lots of yard signs near your home, but with inexperienced agents? You are in control of this decision. Do your research and find an expert online marketer who has a proven track record of marketing and selling lots of homes. I cannot stress this enough—your home is one of your largest assets.

Mistake #3- Hiring a Neighborhood Realtor®

Along the same lines, many sellers think it's important to hire a neighborhood Realtor®. Do you think hiring the local Realtor® will get you the most money and give you a stress-free sale? Does your local Realtor® have advanced training in marketing, business, and negotiations?

Also, does your local agent have experience selling homes in various markets? Can they bring you buyers from multiple markets? This is critical because buyers aren't searching for homes locally anymore. They're searching globally. Neighborhood Realtors® do not have access to more buyers just because their office is near your home.

Think of hiring a Realtor® like hiring a real estate doctor who makes house calls. If you were to need heart surgery, you wouldn't want to go to a doctor just because the doctor was local. You'd seek out an experienced specialty surgeon with a track record of success. You should approach hiring a Realtor® the same way.

Mistake #4 – Hiring a Realtor® Who Gives You the Highest Listing Price

Another mistake home sellers make after interviewing a couple of Realtors® is hiring the agent who says they'll list the property at the highest price. The Realtors® who tell you they'll list your home at a high price know your home won't sell at that price, but they tell you a high price anyway just to get your listing. Then, after three or four months, they suggest lowering the price without implementing any new marketing or doing anything more to attract potential buyers. So you agree to lower the price and the Realtor® quickly puts a price reduced sign on your lawn. I'm sure right now you're so excited to hear that you will be getting a price reduced sign on your lawn. I don't think so! (See Chapter 9: Pinpoint Pricing)

Mistake #5 – Hiring a Realtor® Who Discounts Fees to Get the Listing

You'll find that expert marketers and negotiators are not quick to discount their fees. Expert Realtors® charge a fair fee based on the job. They estimate the cost of selling your home, such as marketing expenses, staff time, and other costs. They also evaluate your situation. For example, if you are selling and buying a home at the same time, they may make an adjustment that could save you some money.

Realtors® who quickly say they'll sell your house for a reduced commission without analyzing the costs might not be planning to spend any money marketing your home, thereby just discounting their time. You should thank them for their time and remove those Realtors® from your list. Yes, commissions are negotiable; there is no set industry fee. However, expert Realtors® do not ***discount*** their fees because they need the business. When you're interviewing an expert for the job of selling your home, he or she is also deciding whether to take the job. For an expert, the decision to work together is mutual.

Consider that if you were selling a $300,000 home, a 1% discount would only save you $3,000. However, you could save up to $30,000 by having an expert marketer and negotiator sell your home, someone who can protect you throughout the entire home selling process and ensure you're not devoured by the Home Selling Sharks.

Now that you know some of the major mistakes home sellers make when hiring a Realtor®, use this knowledge to move forward while at the same time having the mindset I discussed earlier: start earlier than you think you should so you can crush the competition and have buyers lined up outside your property. Keep this at the forefront of your mind when choosing a Realtor®, and make sure your Realtor® has the same mindset too.

Options When Selling: Traditional Realtor® Model vs. Team Model

Essentially, you have two options when deciding to list your home for sale:

Option #1 – Traditional Realtor® Model

In a traditional Realtor® model, the consumer typically suffers. The service ball is dropped because one Realtor® is doing everything. There is no team and there are no experts running the show. How can one person match a team of experts?

Option #2 – Team Model

In a team model, sellers have a group of experts working for them along the customer experience timeline. Nothing falls through the cracks. Hiring a company with a team model allows the marketing and negotiating expert to concentrate on the most important details that keep money in a home seller's pocket. In a team model, the expert marketer and negotiator typically acquires business from past client introductions and referrals.

Regardless of which option home sellers choose, once they're ready to enter into a listing contract, they must protect themselves. It's important to have an easy exit guarantee. This means that if the real estate company isn't doing its job correctly, the listing contract is void after the stated time frame, for example, 30 days. This is essential, especially when working with a friend or family member.

See **www.HomeSellingSharksBook.com** for an example of an easy exit agreement as well as illustrations and videos explaining the differences between a traditional Realtor® and an expert consultant. It is very important before moving on to the next chapter that you understand the importance of hiring an expert marketer and negotiator when selling your home. If you do not hire an expert, you will lose thousands and the next seven strategies will never be implemented properly, or at all. The fact is that these strategies do not even exist in the traditional Realtor® model.

Chapter 4
Strategy #2 for Fighting the Home Selling Sharks: Pre-Marketing Home Inspection

Wouldn't you like to know what, if any, repairs are needed up front so you aren't bitten by the Inspection Shark? Having a pre-marketing home inspection gives you valuable time to make necessary repairs *before* showcasing your home to prospective buyers.

It's important that the pre-marketing home inspector use a magnifying glass and uncover all the repairs needed at this critical part of the home selling process. There are many home inspectors out there and not all home inspectors are the same, so be sure to choose an experienced one. Your expert consultant should know an expert inspector, one he or she uses on a regular basis. It took me about 10 years to find the right inspection company, one that is not only approved by the American Society of Home Inspectors but also experienced in performing pre-marketing inspections.

Once the pre-marketing home inspection is complete, your expert consultant will advise you regarding what repairs should and should not be completed so you don't spend money on unnecessary fixes. The success of fighting the Inspection Shark is having a consultant who will analyze the inspection report and offer advice on what repairs you should commit to doing and which ones to hold off on and use as a negotiating tool.

The pre-marketing home inspection was Leo's next step after hiring us. Leo signed a Coming Soon listing agreement in October with an April on-the-market date. We ordered an inspection a few months before Showtime (the first day the home goes on the market). This allowed Leo time to make all the necessary repairs before showcasing his home to prospective buyers. Since Leo picked from my long list of reputable licensed contractors, this helped him feel comfortable that the repairs would be done correctly and in a timely manner.

Also, we saved Leo money because we had time to negotiate the cost of those repairs. Reviewing the inspection report, we were able to see which repairs were noted as defective, ones that needed to be completed, versus marginal, which may or may not have made sense to complete. Because we had several months before his property was going on the market, we were able to do one repair at a time and not create any stress for Leo.

How can a pre-marketing home inspection, like the one Leo had on his home, work for you? And why is it so important to have a home inspection completed *before* your home goes on the market? As you can imagine differentiating your home from the competition is a key factor in this new world of real estate. Since the Inspection Shark has a big bite, the Pre-Marketing Home Inspection Strategy alone, when used effectively, will keep more money in your pocket.

After teaching thousands of future home sellers, I have learned that they all want three things. They want to sell their home:

1. For the most money
2. In the least amount of time
3. Hassle-free

Let me show you how this one strategy of having a pre-marketing home inspection encompasses all three of these points.

First, let's talk about money. Performing a home inspection before placing your home on the market allows you to make all the necessary repairs prior to showcasing your home to prospective buyers.

After a pre-marketing home inspection, sellers should review the inspection report with their expert consultant and decide what repairs to make to increase the value of their home. Sometimes I advise sellers to hold off on repairs until buyers start submitting offers. If a bidding war ensues, then repairs can be taken off the table during negotiations.

More importantly, you want to make sure the money spent on repairs comes back to you, two to three times your investment. The earlier you start the home selling process, the more time you have to negotiate repair estimates with the contractors. You can also ensure that any completed repairs were done correctly and at the best possible cost.

Also, before submitting an offer, buyers love reading the home inspection report and seeing the seller's list of completed repairs and receipts from the licensed contractors. It's like reviewing a Carfax report for a home. Buyers feel comfortable and they submit a clean offer, at top dollar. In fact, statistics show that most home buyers are more confident buying a home that was pre-inspected since they feel comfortable they aren't buying a money pit.

Now, let's discuss selling in the least amount of time. Experience shows that approximately 50% of the time after buyers read a pre-marketing home inspection report with an organized list of completed repairs and receipts, they won't perform another home inspection. Therefore, this eliminates the 14-21 day contingency period after you sign an agreement of sale, when the buyers have the right to walk away. Now you can start making plans to move to your next destination.

Also, whether the buyers perform their own home inspection or not, all cards are on the table. Offers are submitted within days of a home being placed on the market, versus weeks or months without this report.

Lastly, sellers want a hassle-free process. By using the Pre-Marketing Home Inspection Strategy, you don't need to worry that a buyer will back out after an inspection because all the bugs have been worked out. You can put your home on the market feeling good that you've addressed all of the negative issues that an inspector would find if a buyer were to have the home inspected.

After having read Strategy #1 you understand the importance of having a skilled consultant on your team when selling your home, right? So make sure, right now, you choose an expert advisor who is effectively and consistently utilizing the Pre-Marketing Home Inspection Strategy to maximize your return when selling one of your largest financial assets.

Visit **www.HomeSellingSharksBook.com** to view my video library, download a sample home inspection report with completed repairs, and get more information on my home seller seminar. A pre-marketing home inspection is just one of the many strategies I share at my home seller seminars.

This one strategy alone can save you thousands of dollars!

Chapter 5
Strategy #3 for Fighting the Home Selling Sharks: Photo Showcase

Don't you want your property to be featured online with captivating photos that'll compel buyers to click on your listing and schedule a showing right away? If you want to fight the Photo Shark and draw buyers to your property, you must make sure to follow this strategy from start to finish.

I featured Leo's home with a stunning photo showcase. Since Leo hired me and my team early in the process, we had the opportunity to present the highest version of his home to prospective buyers by hiring a professional real estate photographer to take FABULOUS pictures of the exterior of Leo's home when it looked its best. This guaranteed beautiful pictures of Leo's home regardless of the season the home went on the market.

35

Just like Leo, you want to be sure to have the best exterior pictures of your home, taken by a professional photographer. As mentioned in Strategy #1, you need to hire an expert consultant months to years before you're ready to put your home on the market. Why, you ask? Rarely will your home look fabulous on the outside the day you finally decide to list your home for sale. Therefore, hiring your marketing expert one year before or at least the summer before officially going on the market will allow them to capture the finest photos of your home.

EXTERIOR PICTURES

As I mentioned, fighting the Photo Shark requires showcasing the best pictures of your home's exterior because most buyers today are looking for homes online. And what's the first picture they see online? The exterior photo. If buyers don't like the outside of the home, they won't view the inside, and they'll move on to the next house. The Photo Showcase Strategy, featuring outstanding exterior pictures, is designed to attract buyers even BEFORE a home officially goes on the market in the Multiple Listing Service! (Read more about this in Chapter 7: Marketing & Website Syndication and Chapter 8: Coming Soon Listings.)

Market studies show that if home buyers click through at least three to five pictures on a listing online, they'll continue to click on all the rest.

But if the first few pictures aren't attractive, they'll move on to the next house. That's why you need at least three to five compelling and marketable exterior photos when posting your home online.

Here are seven steps your expert real estate consultant should follow to capture the most marketable exterior photos for your online property showcase:

1. Hire an Expert Real Estate Photographer, Not Just Any Photographer

Thinking of hiring a friend or family member to sell your home, someone who is not an expert in the field of real estate? First, find out if their normal practice is to hire a professional photographer versus using their cell phone to take pictures of your home. It's a known fact that most Realtors® take pictures of their listings with their cell phone. Just look online and you will see. Your home is not going to shine online without professional photos.

An average agent typically only works with buyers and only sells four homes a year. Rarely does an average agent have a seller client listing. Therefore, the Realtor® you're thinking of hiring probably doesn't have a trusted network of professionals, including an expert photographer.

If the Realtor® says, "list with me and I'll hire a photographer for your home," who would the Realtor® call if he or she doesn't have an existing business relationship with a real estate photographer?

Anybody can take a photo, and photographers are a dime a dozen. Everybody knows a photographer, just like everybody knows a Realtor®, a lawyer, and a financial planner. But as we all know, just because someone works in a particular profession doesn't mean that person is a specialized expert or has the high-quality tools needed to excel in their field. The same can be said about photographers. Not all photographers have years of experience dedicated to real estate photography or the equipment needed to deliver the best product.

For instance, only a handful of real estate photographers will spend money on imaging software to enhance photos. It's this magic, which the photographer applies *after* taking the pictures, that makes your home come to life online. Expert photographers will take a couple of hours after a photo shoot to touch up images and brighten them so they look their finest. They will not settle for anything less. However, most photographers will not take the time or use the software to do this. Instead, immediately after the photo shoot, they'll submit a photo disc of images, get paid, and move on to the next house.

Additionally, while most traditional Realtors® save drone photos for million-dollar properties, an expert marketer believes all sellers must have extraordinary aerial pictures to showcase their home. An expert real estate marketer will not stand for anything less than the best and will not accept the unacceptable, especially for the fees home sellers pay when they hire a Realtor to sell their home.

2. Plan for Fabulous Exterior Photos

Preparation is critical to ensure a profitable sale of your home. Therefore, once you have the very first thought of starting your home selling journey, call your expert agent right away. Your consultant will be able to plan the perfect time to have the professional photographer capture your home when it looks its best. The success of your marketing plan depends on preparing your home as well as determining when your exterior photos should be taken. You should plan for the sale of your home as you would any other asset. Unfortunately, sometimes people spend more money and time planning a vacation than they do preparing to market their home.

Normally, a home's exterior looks best in May, June, or July. I usually get hired the spring or summer of the year before the home goes on the market. This gives me time to send my professional photographer to capture photos of my client's home when it looks the most attractive on the outside. Then, we're able to get the most compelling shots that will attract the most buyers.

Consult with your marketing expert about the time of year your home looks its finest on the outside, and prepare to capture magical moments! Here's what my team and I do to guarantee fabulous exterior photos. If the outside of the home looks its best in the springtime with a cherry tree blossoming, we take a picture then. If there's a garden in full bloom in the summer, we take photos of the exterior at that time. If the exterior of the home looks especially magical at different times of the year, we will return as many times as needed throughout our journey to continue to capture the most compelling pictures, saving them until our clients are ready to list their property. The key is to take lots of beautiful exterior photos of your home when it looks it ultimate best.

An outstanding picture showcase taken at the right time of year can make all the difference when selling a home. Imagine two photos: one is of the outside of a house on a beautiful spring day with colorful flowers surrounding the walkway; the other shows a house with a snow-covered lawn and bare trees. Which photo do you think would be more appealing?

Now, take a moment and visit **www.HomeSellingSharksBook.com** and check out Strategy#3: Photo Showcase to see how great exterior pictures make all the difference when marketing a home for sale.

3.   Prepare the Exterior of Your Home

On picture day make sure every facet of your home's exterior is photo ready. Your home should be freshly power washed or painted as well as mulched. Also, if shutters or the front door are faded, they should be painted. Trees and shrubs should be pruned and your lawn should be freshly mowed. Additionally, items that detract from your home's beauty should be put away: trash cans, a Realtor® sign, cars in the driveway, a water hose, etc.

4.   Capture the Best Angles of Your Home

An expert consultant will bring in their experienced real estate photographer to take stunning, crisp photos and, more importantly, take them from the right angles. For instance, the exterior picture of a house should never be taken straight on. Every house has its good and bad sides, just like you. When someone takes your photo, what do you do? You make sure your hair looks good and your clothes are pressed, and you tell the photographer to capture your best angle. "Take the picture from my left side. It makes me look younger." This same preparation and detail is needed when you're having professional photos taken of the exterior of your home.

A skilled marketer knows what angles make a home more compelling online and drive buyers to call about your property. In contrast, photos taken at bad angles will scare away buyers, and your home will never be shown. Remember, if buyers don't like the picture of the outside of your home, they won't click on the rest of the photos, and they certainly won't request a showing.

5. Check the Weather Forecast

Nobody wants to look at pictures of a home taken on a cloudy day! To make sure your professional photos are the best they can be, your consultant will make sure to check the weather forecast and schedule your photo shoot on a sunny day. This perfect natural lighting will allow your home to shine.

6. Select Photos and Store Them Until Ready to Showcase

Once your photographer has taken all the photos of your home's exterior, your consultant will review the pictures and choose the best photos to market later, when your home is ready to list. Keep in mind, the MLS only allows a listing to have about 25 pictures.

As a result, you'll need at least five to six marketable exterior photos so they can be rotated to keep your listing fresh once your home is on the market. The consultant will then store your most marketable photos on a computer until your home is ready for Strategies #5 and #6.

7. Showcase Your Photos

This is an exciting moment, and you've worked so hard to get here! By this point, your consultant has taken the time to ask you thought-provoking questions and clarify your values to understand what's important to you about selling. Based on your answers, together you have created your unique home selling strategy. Part of that strategy is to decide the best moment to bring your stunning images out of storage and showcase them live online on your property's Coming Soon listing. Your expert consultant should have a dedicated website for Coming Soon Listings. Our site is **www.ComingSoonListings.com**, which you'll learn about in Chapter 8.

A fabulous online photo showcase *before* the property actually goes on the market creates buyer demand and compels prospects to request more information about your home. This large demand for your home will drive up the price and have buyers paying you more money than you could ever imagine.

In short, having amazing exterior photographs of your home prior to it going on the market is the most effective way to fight the Photo Shark. (Read more about this in Chapter 7: Marketing & Website Syndication and Chapter 8: Coming Soon Listings.)

Now, let's see how to get compelling interior photos of your home.

INTERIOR PICTURES

Of added importance when fighting the Photo Shark is the interior picture showcase. It's imperative to show buyers the highest version of the interior of your home, especially due to the limit placed on the number of exterior and interior photos posted online, usually 20 to 25. So make sure these are the best pictures of your home and that they'll attract the target market for your property.

Depending on the home, if the first five to six pictures are aerial and ground photos, then you have the remaining allotted pictures to showcase the interior of the home. Make this a fantastic experience for online lookers as well as a profitable one for you.

Capturing the best interior photos involves preparation, effective staging, and professional photography. Let's look at the steps to follow to obtain captivating interior pictures. These steps assume you already hired your photographer using the previous suggestions (see Exterior Photos, Step 1).

1. Determine the Most Marketable Rooms

Because most sellers aren't ready for photos of their home's interior at the time exterior photos are taken, rooms are generally photographed at a later time. However, when the professional photographer is taking exterior pictures, it might be possible to also take photos of certain marketable interior rooms that might be ready. As a result, the first step for interior photos is to determine which rooms are the most marketable for pictures before the home goes on the market.

2. Decide If Any of the Rooms Can Be Temporarily Staged

While the professional photographer is taking exterior pictures of your home, your consultant might decide that some interior rooms can be "fake staged." This involves temporarily moving items out of one marketable room into another so that the photographer can capture photos of the room you've cleared. For instance, you could take everything off the kitchen counter and place it into the dining room to "fake stage" the kitchen for pictures. After the photos have been taken, you can take every item back to the kitchen and return to normal life. Then your consultant will store these pictures until you're ready to market your home for sale, just as they do with exterior pictures.

3. Notify Consultant as More Rooms Become Ready for "Fake Staging"

As you're preparing your home for sale and decluttering, some rooms might become easier to fake stage. You might be donating items to charities, putting things in storage, or just cleaning and organizing. As more marketable rooms become available for photos, contact your consultant so they can capture pictures of those areas. The more interior photos you can have of the most marketable rooms will guarantee more eyes on your listing online during the pre-marketing period. (See Chapter 7: Marketing & Website Syndication.)

4. Complete Interior Picture Photo Shoot

Within one week of the house going on the market, a complete interior photo shoot should be completed and your fabulous pictures posted online. To prepare for interior pictures, sellers should remove certain objects that make rooms look smaller or cluttered, such as throw rugs, knickknacks, soap bottles, items on countertops, etc. These things can be hidden under the bed or in a closet during the photo shoot, though keeping some of these objects out during showings may be fine.

Your consultant will assist you during this process. Also make sure bathroom toilet seats are down, trash cans are put away, and window blinds are open all the way to allow for natural light. It's important to make the rooms being photographed look as inviting as possible so they compel prospective home buyers to call about your property and schedule a tour. Your consultant should give you a complete list of how to prepare for the interior photo shoot.

5. Enhance Photos with High-Tech Software

Once the interior photo shoot is complete, the photographer uploads all the pictures to a high-tech software program, implementing the same technique used to enhance exterior photos. To make the photos look their best, the photographer then spends a couple of hours enhancing them.

6. Decide Which Pictures to Use

Once your expert marketer receives all the interior pictures from the photographer, it's time to decide which ones to use to complement the photos of your home's exterior. Your expert marketer will select the best images, post them online and then blast your listing all over the Internet (See Chapter 7: Marketing & Website Syndication for pre-marketing photo techniques.)

The Photo Shark, if not handled properly, could chomp through thousands of dollars. That's why you should start earlier than you think you need to and hire an expert to get your fabulous photos, so you can crush the competition.

Chapter 6
Strategy #4 for Fighting the Home Selling Sharks: Room-by-Room Review

A room-by-room review is an assessment conducted on your home by an expert real estate consultant. It allows you to benefit from valuable feedback and an action plan designed to set your home apart from the competition. This strategy will evaluate how committed you are to keeping money in your pocket. My question is this: Are you ready to really differentiate your home from your competition? Are you willing to do what it takes?

With Leo, we started the process of differentiating his home by conducting a complimentary room-by-room review and using my Secret Staging Checklist. We went through each room and created a strategy for every area of the home, including the basement and the garage. This strategy included not only the possible repairs needed for each room but also how we were going to present each room to Leo's prospective buyers, both online and offline. Leo understood the need to prepare his property early before listing it for sale.

You might be wondering, what are the benefits of a room-by-room review? Why do you need one if you're not going on the market for three to five years? Let me show you how important it is to know what you don't know about selling and staging your home.

During a room-by-room review, your expert consultant will evaluate the salability of your home and offer ways to prepare the home to go on the market, such as advice on paint colors, staging, decluttering, and so on. It's like having a real estate doctor making a house call for your home, giving you ways to improve your home's value.

Some home sellers aren't aware of how important it is to take advantage of this opportunity months to years in advance of selling their home. They think, "My home isn't ready for this." Your home doesn't need to be ready! As a matter of fact, 100% of my home sellers realized how important it was to have a room-by-room review at least six months to one year before going on the market. Remember it's important that you start earlier than you need to so that you can keep more money in your pocket and avoid being bitten by the Home Selling Sharks.

Sellers who've taken advantage of my room-by-room review say it helps them put together an action plan, offers them hope, and gives them a good place to start. Don't worry if your home is cluttered. A real estate expert can look past the clutter and give you concrete direction on what you need to concentrate on first, second, and so on. Give your home a chance to shine! The room-by-room review process is designed to help you sell your home in 26 days or less, stress-free, and for top dollar.

Let's look at the six steps of a room-by-room review:

1. Design your unique home selling strategy

Every client has a customized strategy because all homes and seller goals are different. Home sellers should work with their marketing expert to design a custom home selling strategy based on what's important to them about selling.

2. Get your list of staging ideas

After understanding and listening to your needs, your expert can now prepare a detailed list of possible repairs or updates to get your home ready for showings. You always have the option to do all, some, or none of them. Some suggestions might include getting the home professionally cleaned, removing any decorative themes, cleaning out the closets, painting rooms, clearing out and painting the garage and basement, removing personal pictures, and taking out unnecessary furniture.

3. Review the list of home inspection repairs

After the pre-home inspection, the inspector will compile a professional report listing all the marginal and defective repairs needed. Go through this list with your expert consultant. See Strategy #2: Pre-Marketing Home Inspection.

4. Get estimates for all suggested repairs and staging

You cannot commit to repairs until you know the cost for each. Get estimates for each suggested repair and staging idea.

5. Decide which repairs and staging ideas to complete

This is a critical moment when you need your expert to assist you in making sure the repairs bring you the most added value. You do not want to spend $2,000 and only get $2,000 back when you sell. Ideally you want a return of two to three times your investment.

6. Hire expert contractors to complete needed repairs

Use the contractors you feel comfortable with or any of the contractors on your consultant's list. Create a home selling timeline with your consultant indicating repair completion dates. Many contractors are slow during the off season. Because you started early, you can save money by hiring contractors when they're not busy. Also, most contractors will discount their services for a job secured in the future.

My team and I provide complimentary 30-minute room-by-room reviews, during which we hand out a free booklet with helpful tips you can use to prepare your home for sale, including my Secret Staging Checklist. Because we're continually learning about new real estate trends and techniques, we regularly update our Secret Staging Checklist online based on current market demands. Go to **www.HomeSellingSharksBook.com** and review Strategy #4: Room-by-Room Review for my most up-to-date home checklist, detailing the latest and greatest techniques for staging your home like a pro.

If you don't have Internet access and would like a copy of my Secret Staging Checklist sent to you, complete the mail-in form in the appendix or call **215-576-8666**. Additionally, you can request a free room-by-room review at **www.HomeSellingSharksBook.com**. We service home sellers in the Pennsylvania counties of Montgomery, Bucks, Chester, Philadelphia, and Delaware as well as in South Jersey. If you live anywhere else in the United States, go to my website, and we will introduce you to an expert in your area.

Chapter 7
Strategy #5 for Fighting the Home Selling Sharks: Marketing & Website Syndication

Do you really expect to sell your home quickly, easily, and profitably without a strategic marketing plan in place designed to reach millions of buyers? To combat the Marketing Shark, you need a marketing expert in your corner who will properly advertise your home and create a strong online presence for your property. A skilled marketer is able to determine your target market in order to get the most exposure for your property. Also, an expert will understand the importance of advertising your property to your target market all over the Internet before it goes into the Multiple Listing Service.

Leo wanted to make sure his home was properly marketed and had an online presence. Our extensive pre-marketing campaign exposed his listing to the marketplace six months in advance of his home's placement on the market, on our Coming Soon Listing website. Using our advanced technology, we were able to see the exact number of hits and the number of unique visitors to his listing. We created demand for Leo's property, which drove up the price, and we sold Leo's home for $21,000 more than the initial Coming Soon price!

How does an expert marketer meet the goal of attracting potential buyers to your property, like I did with Leo's home? Two necessary things come to mind. One, an expert will spend the money needed to attract buyers. And two, the expert will subscribe to a service offering access to statistics from every marketing effort, such as the number of online views, unique visitors to your website, emails, and call leads. Otherwise, how would you know if the marketing of your property is reaching the target market for your home?

Now, let's compare the traditional Realtor's® marketing plan to an expert marketer's plan so you can understand the importance of having a skilled marketer on your side.

A traditional Realtor's® marketing plan consists of the following:

1.   Promise you a high price to get your listing, and sign listing papers with no concrete marketing plan and no easy exit agreement.

2.   Place a sign on the lawn with all calls going to the general office number. Since the sign does not have a direct number to the listing agent, all calls on the property go to the new, inexperienced agent on floor time. Also, the sign is not reflective, meaning it cannot be seen at night.

3.   Give the seller basic tips on how to stage the home, ones that anyone can learn about by reading a book, going online, or watching HDTV. These agents may only sell a few homes each year and usually do not have the experience to give proper advice to separate your home from the competition. Remember, you want to crush the competition when selling your home.

4.   Quickly get the listing into the MLS in hopes that the property sells so they can get paid sooner.

5.   List the home in the newspaper, which people aren't reading.

6.   Post the listing on one website—the company website. Ninety percent of Realtors® do not invest in their own website. They rely on the real estate company they work for to market their homes. Since the company is giving away

70% to 90% of the commission to the agent, the company does not do any marketing either. If leads do come in, all your prospective buyer leads go to the inexperienced agent on floor time.

7. Call you after 30 days on the market to reduce the price because the home is not selling. They tend to avoid taking time to personally meet with you, do a walk-through tour of your home, and review why the home has not sold. Typically, they don't come up with any suggestions for what to do next. They know they have you in a contract for six months, maybe longer, and there is no easy exit from the contract. They lower the price without adding any new pictures, remarks/descriptions, or updated marketing.

8. Put a price reduced sign on the lawn, which shouts to everyone, "What's wrong with me?" Your MLS property listing now has a red downward-facing arrow to indicate a price reduction. Buyers and agents are wondering: How low will you go? **An expert marketer does not even own a price reduced sign.**

Ultimately, traditional Realtors® don't do any pre-marketing because they have no idea what pre-marketing is! What's more, the entire process takes a lot of time and money. As you continue reading, notice that the entire concept of an expert marketer's plan is to have an extensive pre-marketing campaign. This campaign is launched as soon they're hired for the job of selling your home and continues until your home goes on the market.

Why is this process so important? Bottom line, putting a pre-marketing strategy in place determines the demand for your home and attracts the target market. The home's online presence will ultimately drive a line of potential buyers waiting outside your door the very first day your home goes on the market.

Here are the steps an expert marketer takes when creating a pre-marketing plan:

1. Multiple Listing Service (MLS) / Trend Waiver Signed by Seller

In order to implement pre-marketing, your expert Realtor must have you sign an MLS waiver form when you sign your listing contract. This waiver must be signed if your home is not going on the market within three business days of hiring a Realtor®. When signing papers, most sellers are usually not ready to go on the market in three days and aren't ready for showings. And even if they are, they should have at least one week of pre-marketing to create demand.

MLS waivers are unheard of in traditional real estate companies. As a matter of fact, most traditional Realtors® don't even know this form exists. Signing an MLS waiver is a critical first step if you're working with an expert marketer.

2. Exterior Photos

You've already read the chapter on fighting the Photo Shark, so you understand the importance of getting beautiful exterior drone and ground photos to market your home online. While most traditional Realtors® save aerial photos for high-end properties, an expert marketer believes all home sellers deserve to have compelling pictures to showcase their home. Eye-catching exterior photos will set your home apart from the competition, and you'll have more prospective buyers viewing your property online.

An expert marketer will also make use of high-quality photography equipment, such as an SLR camera with a wide-angle lens. They'll hire a photographer who has invested money in a premier software program that enhances photos so that your property can stand out from the competition.

My clients generally hire me a least one year in advance so I can get fabulous exterior photos and drone pictures and store them in my computer until the home is ready to go on the market. I have a Premium Google Earth account, which offers high-quality exterior photos, in case my team and I were not hired early enough and did not have the opportunity to take fabulous pictures of a client's home. Do you think the traditional Realtor® invests all this time and money?

Additionally, if you wait to hire someone to sell your home and then choose to hire a traditional Realtor®, they can only get pictures of what your home looks like at the time you hire them. And chances are that your home's not looking its best. For instance, you might hire a Realtor® in February or March to have your property listed in the spring. But what does the outside of your home look like in February and March? Probably not its finest. I hope by now, the exterior photo concept is starting to sink in.

So now you have great exterior pictures, courtesy of your expert marketer. What's next?

3. Fantastic Property Description

At this stage, professional interior pictures have not been taken yet. As a result, now you need your expert marketer to write compelling details of your home that will draw buyers to your property when it's posted online. Have you read some of the descriptions of homes posted online? Then you know that most are not very compelling!

Your marketing expert should identify the unique features of your home, and then write remarks that tell a story about how these features would benefit potential buyers. The description of your property should leave buyers wanting more information and drive a call to action from your target market. Interested buyers will be eager to see your property and quick to schedule a showing.

4. Website Syndication

Now it's time to show the world your home and invite buyers to take a tour. Since the first showing of your home is online, the initial unveiling of your home must make an impact. If you can't attract buyers online, your home will just sit for months without any showing requests.

An expert marketer will create a personal property website for each seller's home, such as 123MainSt.com. They'll also have the home syndicated on thousands of websites ranking high on search engines. Remember, the purpose of this step is to start showcasing the home to prospective buyers and get them excited to see your home.

5. Review Website Statistics

If buyers like the home, they might call the office. However, they usually send an email or have their agent request more information. The more people who call and click on the website, the more demand there is for the home. This information allows the expert to start negotiating, making sure sellers get full price or more. This is information you'd never have if you used a traditional Realtor's® method. Instead, you'd go into the market blindly and have the potential to lose thousands of dollars. (See the next chapter detailing the Coming Soon Listing system.)

6.   Ready for Interior Pictures

Most of the time the interior of a home is not entirely ready for pictures, though maybe some rooms are. As noted in Strategy #3, the first step for taking interior pictures is to determine which rooms are the most marketable. You have already created demand from the stunning exterior pictures and descriptive remarks, so start preparing the rooms that are most marketable first. This will allow the professional photographer to take photos of those specific rooms. These additional pictures can then be used to generate more traffic to your online listing. Once your home is completely ready, the photographer will take the remaining pictures, and you'll be ready for market!

Let's recap how to fight the Marketing Shark. First, sign an MLS waiver, which allows your expert marketer to post fabulous exterior photos online. Then your marketer will write a captivating property description. Next, get your property syndicated on thousands of websites and capture and review vital website statistics. Lastly, after you've staged your home, have a professional photographer take interior photos that showcase the best features of every room.

Completing these steps *before* a listing goes on the market ensures buyers on your front doorstep the very first day your home goes on the market. More importantly, it guarantees more money in your pocket and your home sold in 26 days or less. That's my promise to you! Will a traditional Realtor® do all of this? I doubt it.

So, which plan do you want—the traditional Realtor's® or the expert marketer's?

Chapter 8
Strategy #6 for Fighting the Home Selling Sharks: Coming Soon Listing

It's crucial that your property be marketed as early as possible all over the Internet to millions of potential buyers. Listing a home as a Coming Soon property *before* it's ready for showings gets buyers excited about your property and eager to view it. If you don't want buyers enthusiastic about seeing your home, ready to pay you list price or more, this strategy is not for you.

My secret formula for selling a home quickly and for top dollar is Eyeballs + Foot Traffic = Home SOLD in 26 Days... GUARANTEED! In today's new world of real estate, only exceptional marketing will get the thousands of eyeballs needed just to get one person into your home. You only get one chance to make a first impression.

How did I get buyers excited about Leo's property? Before I placed Leo's home on the MLS, my team and I sent out announcements to every media outlet we could think of, including social media. This drove up the demand for his property. Buyers and Realtors® were calling every day. Everyone wanted to know when his home was going on the market. Because Leo's home was listed as Coming Soon for six months, there was an abundance of organic traffic to our website and the home popped up at the top of all the search engines. This expert high-tech marketing led to several showings the first day on the market and an offer in two days, over the listed price!

The Coming Soon process is like a trailer for a new movie or a Broadway show. It has the same purpose and effect: to create excitement and demand for people to come and pay money to see the attraction, sometimes standing in line, waiting to be one of the first in the door.

Ultimately, the Coming Soon Strategy drives up demand, allowing sellers to sell their home quickly and for top dollar. Additionally, it gives your expert Realtor® the opportunity to hear buyer feedback firsthand and determine if your home is priced correctly. If a pricing adjustment is warranted, your consultant can modify the price as needed before your home goes into the MLS, in front of millions of viewers. (See Chapter 9: Pinpoint Pricing.)

During the Coming Soon stage, my team and I generate Internet traffic to promote our clients' properties, gaining a strong online presence with our Coming Soon website, **www.ComingSoonListings.com**. We also get viewers from every social media outlet available. In addition to online communication about the new listing that will be coming on the market, we place a Coming Soon sign on the lawn.

A Coming Soon sign on your lawn about 30 days before your property is officially listed for sale lets your neighbors know the home will be going on the market. At the same time, we send a letter from our clients to their neighbors. Our philosophy is that 25% of buyers come from neighbors who know someone who may want to move into the area. Both the sign and the letter generate even more traffic to the website.

So where are you right now in the process? You've hired your marketing and negotiating expert, had a pre-home inspection, had fabulous pictures taken, formed a strategic plan from the room-by-room review, and now your property is marketed on thousands of websites as a Coming Soon listing with a Coming Soon sign on your lawn.

Now it's one week before your property is ready for showings. During the last seven days of the Coming Soon period, you're putting the finishing touches on your home's interior, prepping it for professional photos. The photographer takes a ton of interior shots from the most marketable angles as well as any additional exterior photos that may not have been taken previously. At this point, your property is ready to go into the MLS and ready for showings to start.

In summary, the Coming Soon Listing Strategy is a perfect way to drive eyeballs and then foot traffic. It allows you and your expert marketer to understand the future demand for your home and increases the odds of a full price offer or higher. It also gives you the opportunity to find a buyer before the home even goes on the market.

Chapter 9
Strategy #7 for Fighting the Home Selling Sharks: Pinpoint Pricing

Do you want top dollar for your home? That's where pinpoint pricing comes in. This strategy, meant for accurately and competitively pricing a home, leads buyers to submit offers at list price and higher. Pinpoint pricing is designed to bring you buyers who are ready to submit an offer, close the deal, and start moving in. By contrast, overpricing a property inevitably leads to one or more price reductions. Too high of a price can also mean the difference between a home selling in months versus days. Have you ever thought about how much money it can cost to have your home sit on the market for months? I am sure you don't want this!

I used pinpoint pricing to create demand for Leo's property. He had a three-bedroom home in a neighborhood of four-bedroom houses, and his home was 20 years old with an original roof and kitchen. We really needed to price Leo's home at the market value to create a lot of demand. We set an aggressive price on his Coming Soon listing, and we monitored the stats and phone calls from Realtors® and buyers. The demand was high. Due to this increased demand for the property, we listed the home in the MLS for $10,000 more. We had four offers on Leo's home in two days. Using my expert negotiating skills, we drove up the price another $11,000, and Leo netted $21,000 over the original Coming Soon price.

As you can see with Leo's story, fighting the Pricing Shark requires strategic valuation. Pricing a home isn't just looking at the comparable sales in the neighborhood. In fact, there are specific steps that should be followed:

Step #1: Design Your Custom Home Selling Strategy Before Pricing Your Home

Sit down with your expert consultant and review what's important to you about selling your home. Having the consultant understand your needs will help set the stage for the entire home selling process. Why are you selling and what's important? Is it more crucial for you to get the home sold quickly, to experience a hassle-free sale, or net the most money? Which is it for you?

Step #2: Determine How to Present Your Home to Prospective Buyers

Good marketers price a product based on the features, benefits, and presentation of that product on the shelf or online. This technique applies to real estate marketing too. When preparing to market and sell your home, you and your expert Realtor® must ask and answer some key questions in order to arrive at a price.

How will you present your property online to prospective buyers? Will you be selling your home as-is, or will you be making some changes to enhance your home's features and benefits? If you decide to make some changes, which updates or repairs will be the most cost-effective and bring the most value?

Therefore, before determining your home's value and posting a price online, you need to think with the end in mind. Additionally, you cannot price your home until you have completed Strategy #2: Pre-Marketing Home Inspection and Strategy #4: Room-by-Room Review. Once all the steps in those strategies are complete, you and your consultant can design a custom home selling strategy and then decide on a Coming Soon price.

Step #3: Review Your Home Selling Strategy Based on the Home Value Test

Expert real estate consultants understand factors that can affect the market value of a home. These factors change over the years, sometimes based on trends and target markets. However, in any market, in any era, there are just some things about your home that can't be changed, such as property location, a sloping lot, steep driveway, and busy street.

Because I'm out in the field every day in this ever-changing real estate market, I'm able to stay up to date on changing factors that affect market value. I've created a Home Value Test, which I've included in the appendix. You can also access my most updated Home Value Test online at **www.HomeSellingSharksBook.com**, located under Strategy #7: Pinpoint Pricing.

Look at the test and review the section discussing things you **cannot change** about your home. Does your home have any of these?

Next look at the section of the Home Value Test listing things you **can change** about your home. Some of these involve removing wallpaper, replacing old appliances and utilities, and painting a neutral color throughout, including painting paneling, dark wood trim, the garage, and basement.

Now look at the section of the Home Value Test listing things that you **could change but may choose not to** because they may not be cost-effective. Some of the items on this list include updating a kitchen or bathroom, finishing a basement, replacing asbestos siding, and installing new floors.

Lastly, look at the section of the Home Value Test listing things you **must change** to prevent your home's market value from being drastically affected. Some of the major items include treating the home for termites, eliminating odors from smoking or pets, mitigating mold or radon, and removing knob and tube wiring.

This is why it's so important to start earlier than you think you need to, so you have time to decide which upgrades or changes will ultimately put more money in your pocket. Starting early also means you have time to get multiple quotes for the work you want to complete and find an estimate that fits your budget.

If you haven't already done so, take the Home Value Test. How many points did you score in each section? Scoring only one point could seriously affect the value of your home, depending on which factor it is. If you have several points, you need to call in your real estate doctor right away! When pricing a home, the traditional Realtor® overlooks these factors that affect value, leaving your home overpriced with a price reduced sign screaming "What's wrong with me?"

Step 4: Determine If You Want the 30-, 60-, 90-, or 120-Day Price

When do you want your home to sell? In 30, 60, 90, or 120+ days? Determining your timeframe for selling will help your consultant price your home. If you want to sell quickly, you'll want an aggressive 30-day price that will bring the most buyers from the moment your property is marketed for sale. However, some home sellers aren't in a hurry, nor are they convinced that the 30-day price is the price for their home. They don't mind if their home stays on the market longer than 30 days and are comfortable testing their price *after* the home is listed in the MLS. So they price their home at a higher 60-, 90-, or 120-day price.

Ultimately home sellers have that choice. As an expert marketer, my responsibility is to do the research and provide information to my clients so that they can make an educated decision. The issue with choosing the 60-, 90-, or 120-day price is that market conditions can change and values can drop. If this happens, the home is no longer even worth the initial 30-day price, and you've lost thousands. Keeping up to date on market trends can help you determine if it's a good idea to start with a price that is higher than market value. For instance, though less frequent, in a market that's trending up, you could benefit by keeping the home on the market a little longer and ultimately get a higher price.

Step #5: Conduct a Pricing Test to Determine the Final Listing Price

I'm an advocate of marketing a home at a 30-day price during the Coming Soon period. Why? To drive up demand, it's important to market a property aggressively, which means pricing a home within 3% of the market value. When a home is priced within 3% of the market value, you will get offers in 30 days! How do you know your home is priced within 3% of the market value? Test, test, test! This is where Strategy #5: Marketing and Website Syndication is so critical.

Pre-marketing your home helps determine the demand for your property. If demand is high during the Coming Soon period, you may be able to increase the price of the property when it hits the MLS. If you're getting lots of calls and requests for more information, congratulations! This means you're priced right or maybe a little low. If you're getting a few calls or emails about your property and the stats are lower than normal, this means the home is priced too high and you should lower the price 4% to 6%.

If you're getting very little or hardly any buyer interest from the pre-marketing, you may need to lower the price by 7% to 12%. If your property is generating no interest at all and there are no online viewers coming to your webpage, you'll need to lower your price 12% or more.

As the seller, you have the final decision on your home's listing price. Consider your selling goals and timeframe when determining your price.

Step #6: Review Recent Comparable Home Sales

Most Realtors® price a home solely on comparable sales of similar homes that have sold in the neighborhood, which can lead to several mistakes. One mistake Realtors® make when evaluating price is to use the sold date versus the pending date of a comparable sale. The day the home settled has nothing to do with the price of the home. The date the property went under contract is the date that the buyer and seller came to a meeting of the minds. This is called the pending date.

The pending date is the date that a Realtor® should use when comparing your home to other sold properties. Why? The values may have changed between the pending date and the sold date. Looking at recent pending sales will also tell you if the market is trending up or down. Consider that the average time between when an offer is accepted to when it's actually settled is 60 days. If a Realtor® uses a comparable home that sold one month ago in the analysis, the agent is actually looking at data from three months ago! Anything can happen in three months that can affect the value of real estate, such as stock market or interest rate fluctuations. In reality, the true value of a home is reflected by the amount a buyer was willing to pay for the home last weekend!

Step #7: The Pinpoint Pricing Chart: On-the-Market Price Indicator

The pinpoint pricing chart (see www.HomeSellingSharksBook.com) is very effective in determining the right price for your home if your home has been on the market and you haven't received any offers. By reviewing buyer feedback from all the showings to date and monitoring foot traffic, you can use this chart to determine if a price adjustment is warranted. The pinpoint pricing chart indicates that if there are many showings but no offers, the price is usually off 4% to 6%. If there are a low number of showings, the price is usually off 7% to 12%. If there are no showings or drive-by visits, the price is off by 12% or more. The idea is to price your home at the 30-day price so you have no need for this pricing chart!

The vast majority of qualified, motivated buyers come through a home the first two weeks of a property going on the market. If your home is priced incorrectly from the start, you'll miss out on buyers. In the end, this leads to sellers getting less than the market value of their home, with the Pricing Shark to blame.

For a sale to take place within 30 days, it's vital to select a price that's right on target. Ultimately, the goal of pinpoint pricing is to set a price that will drive buyers to bid on your property. Remember, you want to crush the competition and have buyers lined up outside your door! Now that you know the steps to determine the market value of your home during the Coming Soon period, you are ready for showings!

Chapter 10
Strategy #8 for Fighting the Home Selling Sharks: Saturday Showtime

This final strategy is a critical step in the process of marketing and selling your home. You've come so far and followed all the other strategies with the help of your expert consultant. The inside of your home is now ready to receive the public.

By now, your inspection has been completed and you have a copy of the report at your home, along with the list of repairs. You have your fabulous exterior and interior pictures, and your expert Realtor® has marketed your home all over the Internet. Your room-by-room review has helped you stage your property for showings. Also, your price has been tested and possibly adjusted during the Coming Soon listing period. Your home is now listed in the MLS and agents have started to organize showings. The property is being viewed online and generating phone calls and emails. Now it's time to showcase your home to prospective buyers and allow them inside.

The day of the week to best showcase your home is on a Saturday, that's why I call this strategy Saturday Showtime. Why should you start the showings of your home on a Saturday? Statistics show that the highest foot traffic for showings occurs on Saturdays. By now, prospective buyers have seen the online marketing revealing the Saturday Showtime or Coming Soon date. However, they are not allowed to come in until Saturday. This instills a sense of eagerness in buyers. They can't just tour the property whenever they want. They have to wait in line for the doors to open, just like at an exclusive Broadway show. This type of strategic timing can lead to the negotiation of a sale price even before the home goes on the market.

This was the case with Leo. We posted his home in the MLS on Wednesday, and we started showing his home on a Saturday. This gave us plenty of time all week to build up showings and start generating phone calls. We let the Realtors® know we had many interested buyers. We also suggested their clients bring their checkbooks!

As I demonstrated with Leo's story, an expert marketer knows that timing is a key factor when listing a home for sale. Saturday Showtime gives you a competitive edge in the marketplace. Then a Sunday open house completes the Saturday Showtime Strategy. The Sunday open house sign is placed all over the neighborhood on Friday, and all the buyers looking at the home on Saturday get worried that the home they love is going to be open to the public on Sunday! The really interested buyers, who will pay you list price and more, come to the open house. They see other potential buyers walking through, which creates a fear of loss. Every time this strategy is implemented, the buyer willing to pay the most for your home appears, paying more than they would have without the Sunday open house.

Can you see how effective this strategy is for completing the preparation of your home to go on the market? Because you started early and followed the 8 Secret Strategies to fight the Home Selling Sharks, you've crushed your competition. Saturday Showtime is here, and buyers are anxiously waiting outside your door. They're ready to outbid the next interested person in line and pay you list price or higher. All of your hard work has paid off and you've got your money where it belongs—in your pocket! After all, isn't that what it's all about?

Chapter 11
What Are Your Next
Steps?

Now that you've learned my 8 Secret Strategies for fighting the Home Selling Sharks, you understand that every strategy adds to the bottom line—it's not just one tip that will keep thousands in your pocket. The success of your home selling adventure all starts with hiring an expert consultant who uses the strategies outlined in this book. And just as Leo began researching the home selling process early, if you're a seller who's ready to get started, you should contact an expert marketer and negotiator immediately.

Time is of the essence when it comes to selling a property. Leo's case is a clear demonstration that any home seller can sell a home within 26 days and keep up to 10% more money in their pocket. Although the home selling process takes time, getting a home ready at least six months to one year in advance can give you a competitive edge. It's never too soon to get started!

If you're in my service area, in the counties of Philadelphia, Montgomery, Bucks, Chester, and Delaware or in South Jersey, connect with me today, and I can start designing your custom home selling strategy. If you're not in my service area, I can still help you. I can research and seek out an expert marketer in your area and review my strategies with them to make sure you keep money in your pocket.

What's the best way to get started?

1. **Attend a home seller seminar.**

Just go to **www.HomeSellingSharksBook.com** to sign up for one of my next home seller seminars. You can either attend in person or watch it online.

or

2. **Call me, right now, for a phone consultation.**

Experience the difference hiring an expert marketing and negotiating professional makes when selling your home. Call me and my team at 215-576-8666 or visit my website to schedule a phone consultation to see how I can help you.

Request a consultation or a free room-by-room review today!

www.HomeSellingSharksBook.com
DianeandTeam@CardanoHomeServices.com
215-576-8666

Appendix

Home Value Test

The following list details items and factors that can affect home value, including things you can change about your home, things you can't change, things that could be changed if they are cost-effective, and things you must change before selling.

These are things you cannot change about your home:

The home is not on a perfect lot. Examples include, but are not limited to, a property that is sloping in the back or doesn't have much level land; on a hill with a steep driveway up or down; on or backs up to a busy street or looks directly into someone else's house; has a retention basin on the lot or some other easement; on a flag lot; has eye sore views from inside the house. If there is either one or a combination of issues, deduct 7% to 15% off the value of a home that is on a perfect lot.

The home backs up to a perceived undesirable neighborhood. Deduct 10% to 15%.

The home does not have a basement, and most homes in the area do. Deduct $6,000 to $10,000.

The home is on a busy street. Deduct 8% to 10%, depending on whether it's a buyer's or seller's market.

The home is on a corner lot. This could lower the price anywhere from 3% to 6%.

The home is the largest home in the development. Deduct a percentage depending on the neighborhood and type of home.

The lot is in a flood zone. Deduct 10% minimum, depending on the cost of flood insurance.

The home does not have a first-floor family room and other homes in the development or in the same price range do. Deduct 3% to 8%.

These are things you can change about your home:

The home has paneling. Paint it or deduct 2% to 5%.

The home has wallpaper (a must to paint). Deduct 5% from the value or give a decorating allowance.

The home has not been freshly painted or is not painted a beige or tan. NEVER PAINT A HOME WHITE! A home will appear more attractive and will sell for more if the entire home is painted one neutral color, such as beige. There needs to be a contrast between the walls and the white trim.

The roof is 17 years old or greater. Deduct the cost of a new roof from the listing price or give the buyers a credit.

The heater looks like it has been through World War I and II. Deduct the cost of a heater from the listing price or give the buyers a credit.

The basement has mold and/or there is (or has been) water in the basement. If you don't address this issue, your property could sell for 20% less.

There is dark trim throughout the house, including around windows and door frames. These must be painted white. Deduct 5% to 10%.

There is no central air and you have forced hot air. Get an estimate to install central air, market the home with central air, and give a credit. You could have it installed; however, this is not always recommended. The decision is based on whether you have duct work already installed in the home. If you do, giving a credit is inexpensive, usually between $3,000 and $4,000. If the home does not have ductwork, the cost will rise significantly. The decision is different for each home. Please consult us first before doing anything.

Windows have lost their seal. Most likely you will need to fix the issue or give a credit.

The home has a malfunctioning septic system. If you have a septic system, the mortgage company will require a septic certification. If you have an issue with the septic system, this could cost $15,000 to $40,000 to repair, replace, or connect to sewer. In most cases, sellers cannot give buyers a credit; this needs to be repaired before settlement.

The home has well water. If you have a well, this could affect value if the well fails testing, either for contaminants or inadequate water flow. You will have to repair this or you may consider connecting to city water.

Landscaping could add value to your home by enhancing curb appeal. We suggest different options depending on the situation.

The home has stucco. If you have stucco, my suggestion is to get the stucco tested. The buyers will test the stucco when they do their inspections. However, many buyers will not even look at a home if the home has stucco and it was not tested nor repairs made. Every home and development are different; therefore, in order to be prepared, you should get the stucco tested.

The home has electric heat. If your home has electric baseboard heat, this will devalue your property. It is best to look into the cost to convert to gas or oil heat.

These are aspects of your home you might want to change if the updates and repairs are cost-effective:

The home has asbestos siding. Deduct $8,000 to $12,000 dollars. If siding is not a neutral color, deduct 3%.

The home has outdated electrical. If you have fuses in your electrical panel, update to circuit breakers. If you have knob and tube systems, these should be replaced with updated electrical or give the buyers a credit. Before selling your home, you need to have a licensed electrician provide an estimate on the cost to change from fuses to breakers. Some home insurance companies will not insure a home with fuse.

The home does not have an updated kitchen or baths. Deduct 10% to 30%.

The home has outdated carpeting. Consider replacing with new carpeting or hardwood floors. Have a sample of the flooring in the home to show prospective buyers when they are previewing your home. If you decide not to change the carpet, you can give a credit. However, people do not want to buy a home with worn carpet, even though they know they are getting a credit. They want everything to be done for them when they walk through the home.

The home has hardwood floors under the carpet. Pull up the carpets and get the floor buffed if you know the floors under the carpet are not damaged.

The home is functionally obsolete. For example, there is no bathroom on the main floor. Deduct 3% to 5%.

The home does not have a garage, and most homes in the area and price range do. Deduct 3% to 5%.

These are aspects of your home you must change:

Active termites must be treated. Mortgage companies may also require treatment for inactive termites. Termite treatment usually costs between $700 and $1,800.

The home has radon levels over 4.0 picoliters. Install a radon mitigation system or give a credit, usually between $750 and $1,200.

The home smells moldy or has any level of mold in the house. Costs vary.

The home has a wet basement. You must get the basement waterproofed or you will see a dramatic decrease in the price of your home. The usual cost is between $7,000 and $10,000.

About the Author

Diane Cardano-Casacio is an innovative marketing expert with an MBA in Marketing, and she is in the business of marketing residential real estate. As seen on FOX, NBC, ABC, and CBS on the *Masters of Real Estate* show, Diane shows off her creative ideas with her Coming Soon Listings marketing system. Diane's proven marketing systems guarantee her clients bankable results and an opportunity to keep up to 10% more money in their pockets in a real estate transaction.

Diane's career in the real estate business started when she was just five years old. Diane spent many Sundays at a sample home with her father, Jim Cardano, a licensed broker and custom home builder. She helped her father by giving prospective buyers a tour of the sample home with innocent passion. A born salesperson, Diane was her dad's top sales agent at the age of five.

As a child, one of Diane's most admirable qualities was her competitive mindset. Her desire to excel in everything she did carried her through basketball championships, golf tournaments, a 4.0 GPA in high school and college, and then success in corporate America.

After eight years of feeling trapped by her corporate America job, in 1993 Diane became a licensed Realtor® and took control of her own destiny. However, she never outgrew her competitive mindset, which translated to her becoming Rookie of the Year—selling 15 homes in her first six months as a Realtor®—when an experienced agent only sells an average of four homes in a full year.

Diane's competitive drive pushed her to start her own boutique real estate company, Cardano, Realtors®. Now, her small team of expert consultants have marketed and sold more than a thousand homes with their main focus being to protect their client's real estate asset.

Diane's unique "6 Months Before You Sell" marketing system is called Coming Soon Listings and, when implemented, guarantees to keep your equity in your pocket. Diane holds home seller seminars, teaching the 8 Secret Strategies that home sellers must follow to sell their home four times faster than average and have a stress-free process. Diane's main focus is to maximize her client's net profit by effectively fighting the home selling sharks. The hundreds of success stories are proof that home sellers must be prepared when selling their home by educating themselves about the home selling process.

It is results like these that should compel you to pick up the phone and call Diane when you get the first thought of selling your home, and see if your home qualifies for her Coming Soon Listing system. Call Diane or go to www.HomeSellingSharksBook.com for your free toolkit explaining the eight strategies you must have in place six months before you list your home on the market.

If you are not a PA resident, call Diane and she will introduce you to an expert consultant in your area. Not happy with Diane and her team? Don't worry! You can fire them at any time after 30 days on the market.

Also, Diane and her team hold buyer workshops where first-time buyers can learn how to create a profitable, stress-free home buying process and become educated about the different loan programs available. Diane guarantees that if her clients are not happy with the home they purchased, she will sell it for free if it's within the first year of ownership. With guarantees like that, when selling or buying real estate, you need to go to www.CallDianeNow.com to maximize your profits! Isn't that what it's all about?

Check out Diane's video blog at www.DianesVideoBlog.com for tons of testimonials, stories, marketing ideas, and much more!

Mail-In Form

Name: _____

Address: _____

_____

_____

Phone Number: _____

☐ Questions to Ask a Realtor®

☐ Profile of an Expert Realtor®

☐ Secret Staging Checklist

☐ Home Value Checklist (for the most updated version)

Additional Notes for Diane & Team:

_____

_____

_____

Mail to:
Cardano, Realtors
1021 Old York Road, Suite 401
Abington, PA 19001

Made in the USA
Monee, IL
28 November 2021

82846669R00059